BIBLE BASICS

A FUN AND EASY WAY FOR FAMILIES TO LEARN TOGETHER

JERRY LUCAS — DR. MEMORY™

Doctor Memory™

Learning That Lasts™

Lucas Educational Systems, Inc. – Dallas, Texas

Published by:

LUCAS EDUCATIONAL SYSTEMS, INC.
Post Office Box 794747
Dallas, Texas 75248 U.S.A.

First Edition, September 2000

Printed in the United States of America

Library of Congress Card Number: 00-104330
ISBN: 1-930853-06-8

Lucas, Jerry
Bible Basics
First Edition

Contents

About the Author

As a boy with a very active mind, NBA legend Jerry Lucas challenged himself by inventing mental games to test his memory. At an early age, Jerry realized that being a successful student in school took knowing not only HOW to learn but also HOW TO RETAIN that learned information. He became determined to develop ways to make the learning process EASY, FUN and LONG-LASTING.

Like a farmer who plants small seeds in the soil and carefully tends them so that they grow, Jerry has devoted his life to cultivating ideas and methods for fun and easy memory-retention methods. The resulting methods are now known as **The Lucas Learning System**™ and have earned him the title of **Doctor Memory**™.

Jerry graduated Phi Beta Kappa from Ohio State University. Not only a scholastic achiever, he excelled as an athlete as well. Jerry became the only basketball player in collegiate history to lead the nation in field goal percentage and rebounding for three years, thus becoming the only three-time recipient of the Big Ten player-of-the-year award. This achievement still has not been duplicated or surpassed. Chosen seven times as an All-Pro during his professional basketball career, Jerry was named one of the 50 most outstanding NBA players of all time. Being inducted into the NBA Hall of Fame in 1979 was perhaps his crowning achievement as an athlete.

Recently, Jerry was chosen as one of the five most outstanding college basketball players of the twentieth century by *Sports Illustrated* in its article entitled "Team of the Ages," which appeared in the November, 1999 College Basketball preview issue.

Although Mr. Lucas initially achieved fame and success by his impressive basketball accomplishments, he continues to score off the court as well. Through the years, Jerry has taught his memory-retention system to millions of people either in seminars or through sales of his books. Not only did he co-author the *New York Times* best-seller *The Memory Book*, he also has entertained countless television viewers with guest appearances on TV talk shows during which he dazzled large numbers of studio audience members by demonstrating his ability to meet and remember all of their names.

In total, Jerry Lucas has authored more than sixty books in the field of memory training and learning systems. **Doctor Memory**™ is now widely known and respected as an expert in developing the many methods that encompass his concept known as **Learning That Lasts**™.

I have written this book due to a great need existing in Sunday School classes and homes across our country. Sunday School teachers and parents often attempt to teach children a basic knowledge of God's Word which is necessary to develop a solid Christian foundation, but they don't really know "how" to teach them a way to remember this information because they were not taught "how to remember" during their school years. This book will show the Sunday School teacher, the parent and the child "how" to make the memory process fun and easy. By applying the simple techniques taught in this book, centuries of frustration for the Christian teacher and Christian student alike will have been eliminated. For the first time the teaching and learning process will not be dependent upon boring repetition but on a "system of memory" that has been proven. I will give teaching suggestions and guidelines in the beginning of this book to help anyone who wishes to learn themself or to teach children these simple methods of learning. I often hear adults say things like, " I don't remember anything I was taught in Sunday School as a child." My wish is that once the information in this book is read and applied, this will no longer be the case. Hopefully thousands of Christian families will study this book together and make it a family project. There aren't nearly enough things that Christian families do together anyway! It is many times too difficult for the whole family to study God's Word together due to the difference in ages, but this book eliminates that problem since family members of all ages can apply and understand the teaching contained in the book.

May God bless you as you apply the contents of this book.

In the memory of Jesus,
Jerry Lucas

How Memory Works

It is important that you have a basic understanding of how the memory and learning process works, so you will fully understand why the techniques in this book have been developed.

As children we learn by seeing and identifying tangible objects. Every tangible object that is pointed out to us is learned automatically the instant we understand its identity. At that instant a picture or mental image of the object is automatically and, more importantly, permanently registered in our mind. From that day on every time we think of a tangible object that we have previously identified a picture or image of that object automatically reappears in our mind. It is so automatic that it is out of our control. God has made it so much a part of our nature that it happens without our realizing it, and we can't keep it from happening. Let me prove it by asking you not to do something. Please do not see a zebra in your mind. That's right, do not see a zebra. You saw a zebra didn't you? It's impossible not to see one. That is what I have come to call Automatic Learning™. It is almost impossible to forget tangible objects that our eyes have seen, and our mind has identified.

We learn almost everything this way before entering school and don't rebel from it, because it is such a normal and natural process. But when we enter school everything begins to change. We can no longer use this truly remarkable Automatic Learning™ ability, because now we are called upon to learn information that is not tangible and does not conjure up comfortable pictures in our mind. We begin to struggle with the unnatural, not the natural, because we are asked to learn intangible letters, numbers, words and symbols that have no tangible identity and conjure up no comfortable pictures in our mind. What if a pronoun walked into the room with you right now. Could you point to it and say, "There is a pronoun. I haven't seen one of those in two or three days." Of course not, you have never seen a pronoun. It has no tangible identity. It is a "nothing" in that sense and not a "something" like a tree, a dog, a horse or a barn. So, what were we trying to learn in school? Nothing! You had to try to learn what a pronoun was though, by defining it with other words that had no identity. The life long struggle of trying to learn unnatural, or intangible, information in an unnatural way, that is by constant repetition, had begun.

I realized the difference between trying to learn tangible and intangible objects or items as a child in grade school. I thought it would be hundreds of times easier to learn if I could somehow have a method of changing the intangible letters, numbers, words and symbols I was being called upon to learn by giving them an identity and making them tangible. A seed was planted that led to the development of The Lucas Learning System™. I have not only developed methods of changing any intangible piece of information into a tangible picture, I have also spent my entire adult life creating learning material to make learning anything fun and easy.

The best way to understand the concept is with an example. If intangible information can be made tangible our Automatic Learning™ ability allows us to learn it naturally, effortlessly and quickly. People struggle trying to learn something as seemingly easy as the states and capitals with boring repetition. You will soon see how easy and automatic it is to learn a state and its capital, and more importantly, you will never forget it, because every time you think of it in the future you will see a tangible picture of the state and its capital in your mind as easily and as automatically as you can see an elephant in your mind.

To the right you see a picture of an ark, like Noah's ark, with a can in front of it. The ark is holding a saw in its hand. The ark, the can and the saw form the tangible picture for the state of Arkansas. You can now see an Arkansas. It is no longer an intangible word. It has been changed from a "nothing" to a "something." If you look again you will see that the can is being used as a holding place for the ark to saw a little rock in half. Now you can easily see that the capital of Arkansas is Little Rock. And, more importantly, for the rest of your life every time you think of Arkansas this picture will automatically pop into your mind, and you will see an Arkansas and the capital of Little Rock. You have now learned the capital of Arkansas the same way you learned what a horse was, that is by seeing it tangibly and automatically registering a picture of it in your mind. With The Lucas Learning System™ it is that easy to learn almost anything.

Since it is always easier to remember what can be "seen" rather than what is only read or heard, it is vital to develop a way to picture intangibles. The Sound-Alike Word System™ was just used in the example of Arkansas and Little Rock. Dr. Memory™ used an ark, a can and a saw to picture the word Arkansas. These three words sound exactly like Arkansas, but they are tangible and can be seen.

Most words are intangible and conjure up no picture or pictures in your mind. **Believe** is such a word. You've **never seen a believe**, but it can be pictured easily with the Sound-Alike Word System™. Below you see a picture of a bee with leaves for wings and feet. It is the tangible way to picture the word believe. The word is no longer a "nothing," but it has become a "something" with an identity. Bee-Leave™ is one of Dr. Memory's™ favorite characters. He developed her to help students "see" the word believe and Bee-Leave™ in their own abilities.

The Sound-Alike Word System™ will be used to picture all of the information in this book to make it easy and fun to learn.

The Books of the Old Testament

**Genesis – Exodus – Leviticus – Numbers – Deuteronomy – Joshua
Judges – Ruth – I Samuel**

**II Samuel – I Kings – II Kings – I Chronicles – II Chronicles – Ezra
Nehemiah – Ester – Job – Psalms – Proverbs – Ecclesiastes**

**Ecclesiastes – Song of Solomon – Isaiah – Jeremiah – Lamentations
Ezekiel – Daniel – Hosea – Joel – Amos**

**Obadiah – Jonah – Micah – Nahum – Habakkuk – Zephaniah – Haggai
Zechariah – Malachi**

The Books of the New Testament

Since the last book of the Old Testament leads into the first book of the New Testament, the picture for the first nine books of the New Testament will begin with the **Mallet Kite**, which is the picture for the last book of the Old Testament.

**Matthew – Mark – Luke – John – Acts – Romans – I Corinthians
II Corinthians – Galatians**

**Ephesians – Philippians – Colossians – I Thessalonians
II Thessalonians – I Timothy – II Timothy – Titus – Philemon**

**Hebrews – James – I Peter – II Peter – I John – II John – III John
Jude – Revelation**

What Love Is and Does

In 1 Corinthians, chapter thirteen, we learn what love is.

Love Animals
(they are lovely)

1. A	APE
2. B	BUFFALO
3. C	CAT
4. D	DOG
5. E	ELEPHANT
6. F	FROG
7. G	GIRAFFE
8. H	HORSE
9. I	IGUANA
10. J	JAGUAR
11. K	KANGAROO
12. L	LION
13. M	MONKEY
14. N	NIGHT OWL
15. O	OCTOPUS

**Love is patient – Is kind – Is not jealous – Does not brag
Is not arrogant – Is not selfish or rude – Does not seek its own
Is not provoked**

**Love does not take into account a wrong suffered - Does not rejoice
in unrighteousness – But rejoices with the truth – Bears all things
Believes all things – Hopes all things – Endures all things**

The Twelve Apostles (Disciples)

The sound-alike word for **Apostles** is **Puzzles**, so the picture used to teach you how to remember the twelve apostles will have some jigsaw puzzle pieces in it.

Andrew – Peter – James – John – Philip – Bartholomew – Thomas
Matthew – James of Alpheus – Thaddeus – Simon the Canaanite
Judas Iscariot

The Full Armor of God

The full armor of God is described in Ephesians, chapter six. God gives us His full armor so that we will be able to stand firm against the schemes of the devil. The full armor of God will be pictured by seeing a throne **Full Of Armor**. (God = The throne of **God**)

Here is a list of the full armor of God beginning at the feet and working up with the hands last. This order makes it easier to remember.

Feet – Put the **Gospel** of **Peace** on your feet.
Waist – Put the belt of **Truth** around your waist.
Breast – Put on the **Breastplate** of **Righteousness**.
Head – Put on the **Helmet** of **Salvation**.
Right Hand – **Pick Up** the shield of **Faith** to **Extinguish** the
                   Flaming Arrows of **The Evil One**.
Left Hand – **Pick Up** the **Sword** of the **Spirit**, which is **The Word Of God**.
Prayer – **Pray** at **All Times** in the **Spirit**.

The Ten Commandments

One - Run: You shall **Have** no **Other Gods Before Me.**

Two - Shoe: You shall **Not Have** any **Graven Images.**

Three - Tree: You shall **Not Take** the **Name** of the **Lord Your God** in **Vain.**

Four - Door: Remember the **Sabbath Day, To Keep** it **Holy.**

Five - Dive: Honor Your Father and Mother.

Six - Sticks: You shall Not Commit Murder.

Seven - Heaven - Clouds: You shall **Not Commit Adultery.**

Eight - Gate: You shall **Not Steal.**

Nine - Vine: You shall **Not Bear False Witness.**

Ten - Hen: You shall **Not Covet.**

The Fruit of the Spirit

The fruit of the Spirit are listed in Galatians, chapter five. The fruit of the Spirit are love, joy, peace, patience, kindness, goodness, faith, gentleness and self-control. The fruit of the Spirit will be pictured by seeing a **White Dove** (The **Spirit**) with **Fruit**. Since there are nine fruit of the Spirit, the white dove in our picture will have nine different fruits on a shelf. We will associate the fruit of the Spirit to nine pieces of fruit. The white dove's fruit in alphabetical order are:

Apple – Love
Banana – Joy
Grapes – Peace
Lemon – Patience
Lime – Kindness
Orange – Goodness
Peach – Faith
Pear – Gentleness
Plum – Self-Control

The Deeds of the Flesh

The **Deeds of the Flesh** are recorded in Galatians, chapter five. In this chapter we learn that there are fifteen **Deeds of the Flesh**. The flesh and the Spirit are in conflict with one another. We need to know and recognize the **Deeds of the Flesh** so we can avoid them, because we are told that those who practice these things cannot inherit the kingdom of God. To overcome the **Deeds of the Flesh**, we learn to walk by the Spirit of God by applying the fruit of the Spirit in our lives.

Immorality – Impurity – Sensuality – Idolatry – Sorcery
Enmities – Strife – Jealousy – Outbursts of Anger – Disputes
Dissensions – Factions – Envy – Drunkenness – Carousings

Goals of the New Self*

In Ephesians, chapter four, we are instructed that there are certain things we should do away with or put aside. These are things the Bible instructs us to not take part in after we have come to know Christ. Shedding our old self allows us to put on our new self, which represents our new life in Christ.

Goals of the **New Self:**

Goal 1:
Lay aside falsehood and speak the truth.

Goal 2:
Be angry but do not sin and do not let the sun go down on your anger.

Goal 3:
Do not give the devil an opportunity.

Goal 4:
Do not steal.

Goal 5:
Let no unwholesome word proceed from you mouth. (Or say only what builds people up.)

Goal 6:
Do not grieve the Holy Spirit.

Goal 7:
Put away all anger, bitterness, slander, wrath, clamor and malice.

Goal 8:
Be kind and forgiving to each other.

To picture the **Goals of the New Self**, we will use some football goal posts or **Goals** with a **New Shelf** on them. Each of the instructions for the new self will be associated to the football players between the goal posts on a football field.

*Paraphrased and shortened to make it easier for children to under-stand.

What to Practice to Keep from Stumbling

In II Peter, chapter one, we learn how to keep from stumbling in our walk with Christ. These qualities supply the entrance into the eternal kingdom of our Lord and Savior Jesus Christ.

*Applying all diligence in your faith, supply moral excellence

*In your moral excellence, knowledge

*In your knowledge, self-control

*In your self-control perseverance (perseverance means to be persistent).

*In your perseverance, Godliness

*In your Godliness, brotherly kindness

*In your brotherly kindness, Christian love

*He who lacks these qualities is blind or shortsighted.

The Beatitudes

The next set of pictures for the beatitudes will be associated to your body. As you see the pictures associated to the people in the following pictures imagine that each picture is on your own body. Since you have your body with you at all times, you will always have the beatitudes with you.

Blessed are the **Poor** in **Spirit**, for theirs is the **Kingdom** of **Heaven.**

The bold and capitalized words above will be associated to your **Head** and you will remember them by recalling the clues in the picture to follow.

Key Word – Head

Blessed are those who **Mourn**, for they **Shall Be Comforted.**

Key Word – Eyes

Blessed are the **Gentle**, for they **Shall Inherit** the **Earth.**

Key Word – Chin

Blessed are those who **Hunger** and **Thirst** for **Righteousness**, for they **Shall Be Satisfied.**

Key Words- Mouth and Tummy

Blessed are the **Merciful**, for they **Shall Receive Mercy.**

Key Word – Face

Blessed are the **Pure** in **Heart** for they **Shall See God.**

Key Word – Heart

Blessed are the **Peacemakers**, for they **Shall Be Called** the **Sons** of **God.**

Key Word – Hand (Think of your **Right Hand.**)

Blessed are those who have been **Persecuted For** the **Sake** of **Righteousness**, for theirs is the **Kingdom** of **Heaven.**

Key Word – Hand Again (Think of your **Left Hand.**)

Blessed are you when **Men Revile** you, and **Persecute** you, and **Say All Kinds** of **Evil Against You Falsely**, on **Account** of **Me.**

Key Words – Feet and **Legs**

Head
Eyes
Chin
Mouth & Tummy
Face
Heart
Right Hand
Left Hand
Feet & Legs

Parables

A **Pair of Bulls** will be used to picture **Parables**. A parable is a short story that illustrates a moral attitude or a religious principle.

Pictured below and on the next page are pictures for a parable as Jesus taught it, as well as His explanation, so you can hide it in your heart. Each parable will be identified with its own special picture to distinguish it from all the other parables.

The Parable of the Sower and the Seed

Part 1: The sower went out to sow; some seed fell by the **road**, and the birds came and ate it up.

Part 2: Other seeds feel on **rocky** ground where it did not have much soil; it sprang up but the sun scorched it, and because it had no root, it withered away.

Part 3: Other seeds feel among the **thorns**, and the thorns choked it, and it yielded no crop.

Part 4: Other seeds feel into **good soil**, and they grew up and yielded a crop and were producing thirty, sixty, and a hundred fold.

Jesus' Explanation

Jesus gave this explanation to his apostles when they asked him to explain the parable of the sower and the seed.

Jesus said*:

Part 1: "The sower sows the Word. The ones by the **road** hear, but Satan comes to take away the Word which has been sown in them."

Part 2: "The ones by the **rocky** place hear the Word and receive it with joy, but when persecution comes because of the Word, they fall."

Part 3: "The ones in the **thorns** hear the Word but the worry of the world, deceit and riches choke the Word."

Part 4: "The ones in the **good soil** hear the Word, and understand it and bear fruit, thirty, sixty and a hundred fold."

*Jesus' words have been paraphrased, or shortened, to make it easier for children to understand.

The Parable of the Mustard Seed

Jesus said, "The Kingdom of Heaven is **Like** a **Mustard Seed**, **Which** a **Man** took and **Sowed** in his **Field.** This is **Smaller** than all other seeds, **But** when it is **Full Grown** it is larger than the **Garden Plants**, and it **Becomes** a tree, and the **Birds** of the air come and **Nest** in its **Branches."**

The Gifts of the Spirit

The gifts of the Spirit are listed in I Corinthians, chapter twelve. To picture the **Gifts of the Spirit** we will see a **White Dove (Spirit)** with some **Gifts** or presents at Christmas time.

**Wisdom – Knowledge – Faith – Healing – Miracles – Prophecy
Distinguishing of Spirits – Tongues – Interpretation of Tongues**

Paul's First Journey

Antioch of Syria – Barnabas and Mark went with Paul to Cyprus Salamis – Paphos – Perga in Pamphylia (Mark Leaves)

Pisidian Antioch – Iconium – Lystra – Derbe – Back through the churches appointing elders to Antioch of Syria again

The Twelve Tribes of Israel

You will picture the twelve **Tribes of Israel** by seeing a **Tribe** of people and a fishing **Reel** with the word **Is** on it. (**Is - Reel** = **Israel**)

Judah – Reuben – Gad – Asher – Naphtali – Manasseh – Simeon
Dan (old) **– Levi** (new) **– Issachar – Zebulun – Ephraim** (old)
Joseph (new) **– Benjamin**

The Genealogy of Jesus

The genealogy of Jesus is listed in Matthew, chapter one.

Abraham – Issac – Jacob – Judah – Perez & Zerah by Tamar – Hezron
Ram – Amminadab – Nahshon – Salmon – Boaz by Rahab
Obed by Ruth – Jesse – King David

**King David – Solomon by the wife of Uriah – Rehoboam – Abijah
Asa – Jehoshaphat – Joram – Uzziah – Jotham – Ahaz – Hezekiah
Manasseh – Amon – Josiah – Jeconiah**

**Jeconiah – Shealtiel – Zerubbabel – Abiud – Eliakim – Azor – Zadok
Achim – Eliud – Eleazar – Matthan – Jacob – Joseph – Mary – Jesus**

Doctor Memory™ Web Site

To enter the Doctor Memory™ web site go to:

http://www.doctormemory.com

Other Doctor Memory™ Products

All Dr. Memory™ products use the Lucas Learning System™ where visually reinforced association models make learning fun and easy. Dr. Memory™ teaches Learning That Lasts™. Please visit the web site at www.doctormemory.com for up-to-date information on the complete product line. Included are descriptions of the complete Learning That Lasts™ product line, as well as actual demonstrations. Excerpts of many of the products are available free of charge also. Doctor Memory™ revolutionary products are available for purchase at doctormemory.com and bookstores. These products include the following:

Adult - Young Adult General Interest

Doctor Memory's™
Picture Perfect Spanish
A Survival Guide to Speaking Spanish

Doctor Memory's™ Learning That Lasts™ methodology is adapted to learn more than 600 "Survival" words required for basic communication of the Spanish language. Careful attention has been paid to insure that the most critical words are taught and that each word is associated with the English equivalent in a way that guarantees accurate pronunciation. In this course, the Spanish language is explored primarily through commonly used words. The addition of basic sentence structure, common phrases and sentences complete the materials; which are designed to prepare the reader to speak the Spanish language more thoroughly than that which is typically covered in a one-year Spanish foreign language course. In addition to teaching over 600 words this book teaches phrases, sentences and basic rules of sentence structure required to speak Spanish.

Doctor Memory's™
Comprehensive Picture Perfect Spanish
Your Reference to the Spanish Language

Doctor Memory's™ Learning That Lasts™ methodology is adapted to aid in the memorization of over 1,600 of the most commonly used Spanish words in this four-volume set. Careful attention has been paid to insure that each word is associated with the English equivalent in a way that guarantees accurate pronunciation. This comprehensive reference teaches words, more detailed grammar, basic sentence structure, conjugation of verbs and more while also exploring common phrases and sentences typical of the Spanish language.

Doctor Memory's™
Names and Faces Made Easy
The Fun and Easy Way to Remember People

The Jerry Lucas technique for remembering names and faces revealed! This unique product tailors Doctor Memory's™ Learning That Lasts™ methodology to aid in remembering the first and last names of those you meet. This method has enabled Mr. Lucas to meet, remember, and correctly pronounce the names of more than 500 people at a time in live studio audience environments. The technique has been successfully taught to hundreds of thousands of people, including numerous Fortune 500 companies. While based on teachings in the best selling *The Memory Book*, the material covered here is far more detailed and comprehensive. Previously available only through exclusive guest appearances and live seminars, this fun and easy technique can now be purchased in either a book or videotape format.

Doctor Memory's™
Learning How to Learn
The Ultimate Learning and Memory Instruction

Doctor Memory's™ unique learning methodology is taught in detail in this comprehensive follow-up to the best selling *The Memory Book* that was co-authored by Mr. Lucas in 1973. *Learning How to Learn* teaches the reader how to apply the Learning That Lasts™ methodology to any subject matter. All eight tools of learning developed by Jerry Lucas are taught in detail. Hundreds of applications are discussed and illustrated. Taking almost 30 years to compile, this is the most innovative and comprehensive learning instruction book ever written!

Childrens' Educational Products

Doctor Memory's™
Ready Set Remember
States & Capitals and The Presidents

Doctor Memory's™ unique Learning That Lasts™ methodology is adapted to children's social studies to instruct the memorization of the states, their capitals, and the presidents of the United States. This book with accompanying audio cassettes will guide the learning process and is ideal for either self-directed students or for use in a more traditional classroom environment. An interactive computer based training version is currently under development and will include animation to assist in learning the geographic location of each state as well.

Doctor Memory's™
Grammar Graphics & Picture Perfect
Punctuation - Volume I

Designed for students, teachers, and adults, this first in an eight volume series includes fun and unique pictures that "lock in" the application and usage of the fundamental rules of grammar and punctuation. Doctor Memory's™ revolutionary learning methodology makes even grammar and punctuation fun and easy to learn.

Doctor Memory's™
Ready Set Remember The Times Tables

Doctor Memory's™ unique learning methodology is adapted to assist in the memorization of the times tables from 2x2 to 12x12. This book teaches a simple and fun method of seeing numbers tangibly. Each problem is then pictured in a unique way in order to differentiate it from the others.

For Families that Wish to Study
the Bible Together

Doctor Memory's™
Bible Memory Made Easy

Doctor Memory's™ unique Learning That Lasts™ methodology is adapted to help students of any age to better understand and remember Bible facts in this eight volume video tape series. Students learn the Books of the Bible, the Ten Commandments, the Fruit of the Spirit, selected Bible verses, Gifts of the Spirit, and much more. Just by watching and listening you will learn and remember many of the important teachings of the Bible!

Doctor Memory's™
View-A-Verse™
Bible Verse Learning Program

Doctor Memory's™ unique Learning That Lasts™ methodology has been adapted to help students of all ages memorize Bible verses simply and easily by seeing the verses tangibly on learning cards that can be reviewed much like everyday flash cards. However, since the verses are pictured and associated with common everyday objects, two amazing things will happen. First, the verses are easily learned and memorized. Second, when the commonly used everyday objects are seen in real life, the verses will be automatically remembered bringing the Word of God to mind throughout the day! Learning Bible verses has never been so easy or fun.

Soon to be Released Products for Reading and Writing

Doctor Memory's™
Alphabet Friends™

Doctor Memory's™ unique Learning That Lasts™ methodology is adapted to children's reading and writing in this alphabet and phonetic sound recognition program. Each letter is pictured graphically so as to guarantee the student learns to recognize and write upper and lower case shapes. All possible sounds made by each letter are pictured tangibly, so the student can see and never forget them. This revolutionary product is the first ever published that allows students to actually see all of the sounds tangibly. The student also learns how to read words that include the basic sounds. An interactive computer based training version will be available as well as traditional workbooks with instruction manuals.

Doctor Memory's
See and Know Picture Words™ Reading Program

Doctor Memory's™ unique Learning That Lasts™ methodology is adapted to children's reading in this sight word recognition program.. Two hundred twenty words (220) make up 75% of what students will read through the sixth grade and 50% of all words an adult will read throughout their lifetime. All of these "sight" words are pictured graphically to guarantee the student learns the words permanently. Recognition of all significant sounds made within the English language are also taught, including silent letters, letters that change sounds, and the common consonant sound combinations such as "ch" and "th". After completing this course the student will tangibly see and know every sound in the English language while being able to read and pronounce new words. Doctor Memory's™ Alphabet Friends™ is a pre-requisite to this program which will be available in a computer based training version or a more traditional workbook with accompanying instruction manual.

Give the gift of Learning That Lasts™
to your family, friends, and colleagues.

Check with your favorite bookstore or place your order
by logging onto our website.

www.doctormemory.com

FOR MAIL ORDERS, PLEASE COMPLETE THIS ORDER FORM:

☐ **YES**, I want _____ copies of **Bible Basics** at $21.95 each, plus $5.95 shipping and handling for U.S. orders (or $9.70 shipping and handling for foreign orders). Non-U.S. orders must be accompanied by a postal money order in U.S. funds. Please allow 3-4 weeks for delivery within the United States and 6 weeks for delivery elsewhere.

**Call the toll-free phone number noted below
for assistance with completing this order form.**
(please note: we cannot accept cash, personal checks or C.O.D.'s)

Check One:

☐ Money Order or ☐ Cashier's Check (payable to Lucas Educational Systems, Inc.)
☐ Visa   ☐ Master Card   ☐ Discovery   ☐ American Express

Bible Basics @ $21.95 per book   = $_____
Add appropriate shipping charge (as noted above)   = $_____
Add applicable sales tax*   = $_____
                           TOTAL PAYMENT   = $_____
                 Include sales tax where required.

Ship to: (please print)

Name_____
Organization_____
Street Address_____
City/State/Zip_____
Phone_____E-Mail_____
Credit Card #_____Exp. Date_____
Signature_____

***For mailing instructions call our
toll free order hot line:***
1-877-479-6463

1-930853-06-8